BEGINNER
BUSINESS VENTURE
WORKBOOK

T0346860

Roger Barnard & Jeff Cady

OXFORD
UNIVERSITY PRESS

Great Clarendon Street, Oxford OX2 6DP

Oxford University Press is a department of the University of Oxford.
It furthers the University's objective of excellence in research, scholarship,
and education by publishing worldwide in

Oxford New York

Auckland Cape Town Dar es Salaam Hong Kong Karachi
Kuala Lumpur Madrid Melbourne Mexico City Nairobi
New Delhi Shanghai Taipei Toronto

With offices in

Argentina Austria Brazil Chile Czech Republic France Greece
Guatemala Hungary Italy Japan Poland Portugal Singapore
South Korea Switzerland Thailand Turkey Ukraine Vietnam

OXFORD and OXFORD ENGLISH are registered trade marks of
Oxford University Press in the UK and in certain other countries

ISBN: 978 0 19 457806 6

Printed in China

This book is printed on paper from certified and well-managed sources.

ACKNOWLEDGEMENTS

*The publisher would like to thank the following for their kind permission to reproduce
photographs*: Alamy Images pp.29 (Office after hours/Richard Peters), 49 (Airline
ticket agent/David R. Frazier Photolibrary, Inc.), 54 (Publishing house newsroom/
imagebroker); Bose Ltd p.20 (MP3 doc), Corbis p.43 (Vesak Bochea ceremony/
Chor Sokunthea/Reuters); Getty Images pp.4 (Businessman signing in for
conference/Ben Bloom/Stone), 9 (Museum/Panoramic Images), 19 (Businessman in
meeting/Michael Hitoshi/Taxi Japan), 34 (Businesswoman in meeting/Michael
Hitoshi/Taxi Japan), 43 (fireworks over the Eiffel Tower/Loic Venance/AFP),
44 (Couple reading map/Henrik Sorensen/Taxi), Photolibrary pp.14 (Businessman
checking watch/Chris Ryan/OJO Images), 39 (Businesswoman on phone/
Amanaimages), 43 (turkey dinner/Radius Images), 60 (cafe/Cultura); PunchStock
pp.7 (hotel reception/beyond fotomedia), 18 (man on mobile/Fuse), 24 (Business
associates shaking hands/PhotoAlto Agency), 59 (Couple eating spring rolls/
blue jean images).

Cover: Getty Images (PhotoAlto/Eric Audras).

Illustrations by: Peter Bull pp.10, 11, 44 (maps), 45; Mark Draisey pp.26, 28, 50;
Mark Duffin pp.23 (all), 30, 31.

Contents

Checking in

Registration

Complete the two conversations at a business conference registration desk. Use the lines below.

> Ah, yes, Ms. Gibson. Here's your name tag and conference bag.
> Thank you.
> Good morning. I'm Nathan Welsh. I'm with Dell.
> Good afternoon.

Conversation 1

A *Good morning.*

B _____ 1

A *Just a moment, please. Yes, Mr. Welsh. This is your name tag.*

B _____ 2

Conversation 2

A _____ 3

B *Good afternoon. My name's Gibson. Amanda Gibson. I'm with NEC.*

A _____ 4

B *Thanks.*

Greetings

Write one expression for each time.

> Good morning.   Good afternoon.   Good evening.   Good night!   ~~Hello.~~

1 _____   2 _____   3 Hello.   4 _____   5 _____

7:30 p.m.   10:45 p.m.   3:15 p.m.   10:00 a.m.

1 Write a self introduction for each person.

1
Jane Carr

2
Jia Liu

3
Da-Ye Kim

4
Richard Harvey

1 _My name's Carr. Jane Carr._

2 _____

3 _____

4 _____

2 Introduce yourself in the same way.

_____

MODULE 1.4

Letters of the alphabet

1 Write these company names as initials.

1 British Petroleum   BP

2 Entertainment Sports Programming Network   _____

3 Fabbrica Italiana Automobili Torino   _____

4 Hewlett-Packard   _____

5 His Master's Voice   _____

6 International Business Machines   _____

7 Nippon Electric Company   _____

8 Tokyo Denki Kagaku   _____

2 Look at this:

ANA is a Japanese company. The initials ANA stand for All Nippon Airways.

Write about another company name that uses initials.

_____

_____

_____

I'm with TDK

1 Write a sentence for each person. Use *I'm with …* or *I work for …*.

1
Kenneth Lee
Cathay Pacific

2
Maria Price
CNN

3
Chae-Hyeon Park
Daewoo

4
Mike Stein
Starbucks

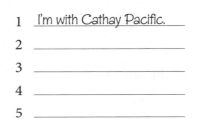

1   I'm with Cathay Pacific.
2   _____
3   _____
4   _____
5   _____

5
Toshi Ono
UPS

2 Write a similar sentence about yourself.

_____

MODULE 1.6

Spelling a name

Write the questions in the conversation. Use the questions below.

And your given name?	~~Could you tell me your family name, please?~~
Is that C-A-R-L?	Could you repeat that, please? Is that L-E-A-V-I-T?

A   Could you tell me your family name, please?   1
B   *Leavitt.*
A   _____   2
B   *Leavitt.*
A   _____   3
B   *No, it's L-E-A-V-I-T-T.*
A   _____   4
B   *Carl.*
A   _____   5
B   *Yes, that's right.*
A   *Thank you.*

MODULE 1.7

Complete the conversation. Use the words below.

are	~~can~~	is	please	spell	that

A *Good afternoon, sir. How* can¹ *I help you?*
B *I reserved a car for two days. My name* _____² *Mendez. Carlos Mendez.*
A *I'm sorry, how do you* _____³ *that?*
B *M-E-N-D-E-Z.*
A *Yes,* _____⁴*'s fine, Mr. Mendez.*
   May I see your driver's license, _____⁵*?*
B *Yes, here you* _____⁶*.*

MODULE 1.8

Write the words in each sentence in the correct order.

1 you   that,   Could   please   spell   ?
   Could you spell that, please ?

2 fill out   card,   you   please   Could   this   ?
   _____

3 key card   your   Here's
   _____

4 over there   The   are   elevators
   _____

5 a   stay   pleasant   Have
   _____

MODULE 1.9

On the phone – I'd like to speak to …

Pierre Durand calls Emiko Takahashi at TKE Engineering. Number the lines of the conversation in the correct order.

Pierre	*Hi, Emiko. It's Pierre.*	8
Receptionist	*Just one moment, please, Mr. Durand. I'll put you through.*	☐
Pierre	*I'd like to speak to Emiko Takahashi, please.*	☐
Pierre	*Thank you.*	☐
Receptionist	*Good morning, TKE Engineering. How can I help you?*	1
Emiko	*Hello, Emiko Takahashi speaking.*	☐
Pierre	*Durand. Pierre Durand.*	☐
Receptionist	*Your name, please?*	☐

MODULE 1.10

Culture corner – Names

1 You meet some people at a company barbecue. Number the speakers 1–5 to match the names. Then check your answers on page 65.

1 Elizabeth Rahman
2 Ja-Cheol Lee
3 Margaret Chang
4 Richard Rossi
5 William Coleman

a Hi! I'm Dick. ☐

b Hello. My name's Betsy. 1

c Afternoon. I'm Bill. ☐

d Good afternoon. My name's Meg. ☐

e Hi there. I'm JC. ☐

2 Write your own greeting. If you don't have a nickname, think of one.

_____

_____

_____

2

At a trade fair

MODULE 2.1 | Where's booth 19?

Complete the conversations. Use the words below.

| Excuse | Aisle | Great | Thank | ~~Where's~~ | café |

Conversation 1
A *Pardon me.* <u>Where's</u> ¹ *booth 19?*
B *It's in Aisle A, on the left.*
A _____² *you.*

Conversation 2
A _____³ *me. Where's booth 82?*
B *Let's see, 82 … It's in* _____⁴ *D, on the right.*
A *Thanks a lot.*

Conversation 3
A *Excuse me, I'm looking for booth 37.*
B *Yeah, it's in Aisle B, across from the* _____⁵*.*
A _____⁶*. Thanks.*

MODULE 2.2 | Numbers 1–99

Write the numbers in words. Use the words on the right.

1	2	<u>two</u>	forty-five
2	12	_____	ninety-nine
3	20	_____	seventy-eight
4	13	_____	thirteen
5	30	_____	twelve
6	45	_____	twenty
7	78	_____	~~two~~
8	99	_____	thirty

MODULE 2.3

Write the answers for the questions. Use the phrases below.

across from the stairs
~~near the elevator~~
on the left, next to the stairs
on the right, next to the restrooms
between the stairs and the elevator

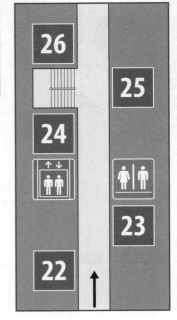

1 Where's booth 22?

It's _near the elevator_ .

2 Where's booth 23?

It's _____

_____ .

3 Where's booth 24?

It's _____

_____ .

4 Where's booth 25?

It's _____

_____ .

5 Where's booth 26?

It's _____ .

MODULE 2.4

1 Read the conversation.

A *Where's your booth?*
B *It's in Aisle D. It's on the left, across from the elevator.*
A *Ah. Booth 86?*
B *That's right.*

2 Write a similar conversation about booth 75.

A *Where's your booth?*

_____

B _____

_____

_____

A _____

B _____

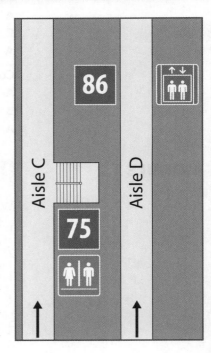

Where's the restaurant?

Write about the locations of four of the places in the Tower Hotel.

USEFUL LANGUAGE

across from	between … and …
near	next to
on the left	on the right

Examples

The business center is on the left, next to the bookstore.

The restrooms are between the business center and the elevators.

1 _____

2 _____

3 _____

4 _____

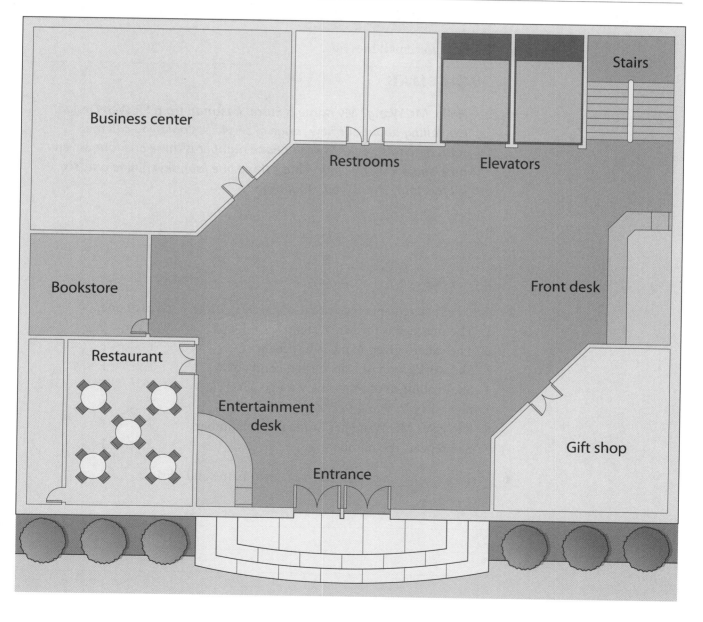

Phone numbers

1 Write the missing words in each phone number.

1 338 620 7621 "three three eight, six two oh, _____ six two one"

2 571 309 6664 "five seven one, three zero nine, _____ six six four"

2 Write your phone numbers in the same way.

office: _____

" _____ "

home: _____

" _____ "

cell: _____

" _____ "

Voicemail

1 Read the voicemail message.

VOICEMAIL

Hello. Mr. Wang? My name is Susan Eastman from SR Web Design. I'm calling about our new range of services. Could you call me sometime this week? My cell phone number is three one four, seven nine one, six six five four. That's three one four, seven nine one, six six five four. Thank you. Goodbye.

2 Are these statements true or false? Circle T or F for each one.

1 The message is for Mr. Wang.   (T)   F
2 The caller's given name is Eastman.   T   F
3 She works for a website design company.   T   F
4 She's calling about their new range of services. T   F
5 She asks Mr. Wang to call her today.   T   F
6 She gives Mr. Wang her home phone number.   T   F
7 She repeats the number.   T   F

3 Write a similar message. Use your own name and ideas.

_____

_____

_____

_____

MODULE 2.8

Write the words in each sentence in the correct order.

1 please   your   have   I   name,   Could

_____?

2 cell phone   What's   number   your

_____?

3 that,   you   Could   please   repeat

_____?

4 spell   do   How   that   you

_____?

MODULE 2.9

On the phone – Where are you?

Kazuo Tamura and Jane Bennett are speaking on their cell phones. They want to meet in the Event Hall at the Miami Trade Fair. Number the lines of the conversation in the correct order.

Jane	*Can you see the restaurant?*	☐
Jane	*I'm in the restaurant. I just got here.*	☐
Jane	*Hello, Kazuo?*	1
Kazuo	*Yes, I can. And I can see you! Bye!*	☐
Kazuo	*Hi, Jane. Sorry I'm late. Where are you?*	☐
Kazuo	*Yes, I'm in the meeting area.*	☐
Jane	*It's next to the café. Are you in the Event Hall?*	☐
Kazuo	*Where is the restaurant?*	☐

MODULE 2.10

Culture corner – Lucky and unlucky numbers

Write answers to the questions.

1 What is a lucky number in your country?
A lucky number in my country is _____.

2 What is an unlucky number in your country?
An unlucky _____.

3 What is your cell phone number?
My _____.

4 What is your favorite number? Why?

_____
_____
_____

Schedules

MODULE 3.1

When's the meeting?

Complete the conversations. Use the words below.

| ~~planning~~ morning call o'clock time afternoon Thursday What |

Conversation 1

A When's the _planning_ [1] meeting?

B Friday _____ [2], at 9:30.

A Great. Thanks.

Conversation 2

A Is the conference _____ [3] tomorrow?

B Yes, at two _____ [4].

A Right. Thanks a lot.

Conversation 3

A Hi, Jim. What _____ [5]'s the sales meeting Tuesday?

B It's in the _____ [6], at three o'clock.

A OK, thanks.

Conversation 4

A Is the presentation Wednesday morning?

B No, it's _____ [7] morning.

A _____ [8] time?

B Ten o'clock.

A Thanks.

MODULE 3.2 — Meetings

Find eight kinds of meetings in the word square.

```
(S  A  L  E  S)  X  P  M  P
 T  S  C  I  O  C  E  I  R
 A  E  U  T  S  M  Y  O  O
 F  P  W  E  E  K  L  Y  J
 F  U  O  A  C  U  C  S  E
 Z  C  M  M  T  I  P  E  C
 E  I  C  L  I  E  N  T  T
 P  Y  S  U  O  P  Z  I  M
 M  P  L  A  N  N  I  N  G
```

MODULE 3.3 — Days of the week

In reports, schedules, and notes, you can write the short forms of the days of the week:

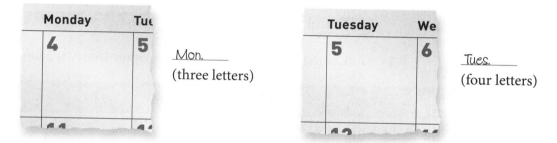

Mon.
(three letters)

Tues.
(four letters)

Write the short forms of the other days of the week. Then check the answers on page 66.

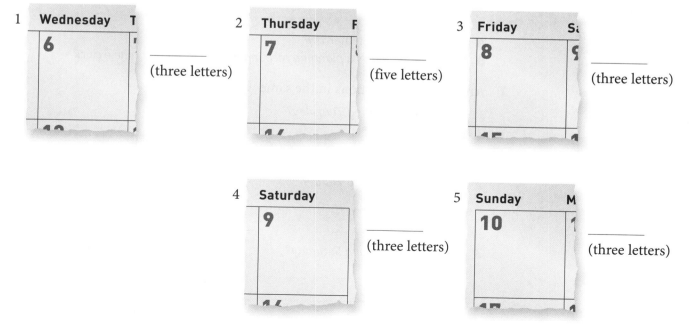

1 Wednesday
(three letters)

2 Thursday
(five letters)

3 Friday
(three letters)

4 Saturday
(three letters)

5 Sunday
(three letters)

MODULE 3.4   Clock times

1   Write these times as digits.

    1   four o'clock   <u>4:00</u>

    2   two fifteen   _____

    3   eleven twenty-five   _____

    4   seven twenty   _____

    5   one forty-five   _____

    6   six oh five   _____

2   Write these times in words.

    1   5:00   <u>five o'clock</u>

    2   5:15   _____

    3   8:25   _____

    4   3:10   _____

    5   9:45   _____

    6   10:05   _____

MODULE 3.5   Schedules

1   Look at the schedule and the conversation. Today is Monday.

Schedule

Tuesday	20	Wednesday	21	Thursday	22	Friday	23	Saturday	24
9:00 a.m. Planning meeting		3:30 p.m. Sales meeting		9:30 a.m. Section meeting		2:15 p.m. Production meeting		–	

A   *Is there a meeting tomorrow?*

B   *Yes, there is. There's a planning meeting in the morning at nine o'clock.*

2   Answers these questions in the same way.

    1   **A**   *Is there a meeting Thursday?*

       B   _____

       _____

    2   **A**   *Is there a meeting Friday?*

       B   _____

       _____

    3   **A**   *Is there a meeting Saturday?*

       B   _____

       _____

MODULE 3.6

A visit schedule

1 Match the words and phrases.

1	buffet	___ demonstration
2	factory	_1_ lunch
3	meet and greet	___ presentation
4	PowerPoint	___ session
5	product	___ speech
6	welcome	___ tour

2 Complete the visit schedule below. Use the events above and decide the times.

Ellis Moldings visit schedule

TIME	EVENT

MODULE 3.7

Visitors

1 Read part of an inter-departmental e-mail.

✉ **E-mail**

As you know, a group from Sony is visiting us tomorrow. This is the schedule. First, there is a meet and greet session at 9:30 and a welcome speech by Monica Weber. Then there is a presentation about our company by Kurt Meyer. After that, there is a factory tour. There is an informal buffet lunch in the company restaurant at 12 noon.

2 Use your own ideas to write a similar e-mail about a visit to your company.

✉ **E-mail**

MODULE 3.8

On the phone – Can I call you back?

Naomi Taylor calls her co-worker, Steve McCann. Number the lines of the conversation in the correct order.

Naomi	*Hello, Steve. Am I calling at a bad time?*	☐
Steve	*Around 3:15?*	☐
Steve	*Hi, Naomi?*	1
Naomi	*Oh, I'm sorry.*	☐
Steve	*That's OK, but can I call you back?*	☐
Naomi	*Sure, that's fine. Speak to you then. Bye.*	☐
Steve	*Well, I'm in a presentation right now.*	☐
Naomi	*Sure, no problem. What time?*	☐

MODULE 3.9

Culture corner – The right time

Read the sentences.

You have an appointment at a client's office at 9:30 a.m.
<u>A good time to arrive is 9:20 a.m.</u>

Write similar sentences for these situations.

You have a sales meeting at 10:00 a.m. in the meeting room.

_____

You are giving a presentation at 2:00 p.m. in the presentation room.

_____

A client invites you to his home for dinner. Dinner is at 8:00 p.m.

_____

4

Companies

MODULE 4.1

Three people are talking about their companies. Complete the information. Use the words below.

countries	factories	famous	has	in
Japanese	makes	with	~~work~~	

> Good morning. I _work_¹ for Nokia. Nokia is a major Finnish company.
> It _____² cell phones. The head office is in Keilaniemi, near Helsinki.
> It has factories in China, Hungary, and other _____³. I work at the head office.

> Good afternoon. I'm _____⁴ Mazda Motor Corporation. Mazda is a large _____⁵
> company. It makes cars, trucks, and vans. The head office is in Fuchu, near Hiroshima. It
> has _____⁶ in Japan and many other countries. I work at the Valencia factory, in Spain.

> Hi. I work for Louis Vuitton. Louis Vuitton is a _____⁷ French company. It makes
> luxury goods, such as bags, shoes, and sunglasses. The head office is in Paris. It _____⁸
> many stores around the world. I work at the Fifth Avenue store _____⁹ New York.

My company

1 Read the text.

Hi, my name's Eileen Lennon. I work for Bose Corporation. Bose is a well-known American company. It makes audio equipment. The head office is in Framingham, near Boston, Massachussetts. It has three factories in Massachussetts, and factories in Canada, Ireland, and Mexico. It has many retail stores in the United States and other countries. I work at the Carrickmacross factory in Ireland.

2 Write answers to the questions. Choose from the short answers below.

Yes, she does. / No, she doesn't. Yes, it does. / No, it doesn't.	Yes, she is. / No, she isn't. Yes, it is. / No, it isn't.

1 Does Eileen work for Bose? _Yes, she does._

2 Is Bose a Canadian company? _____

3 Is it well-known? _____

4 Does it make audio equipment? _____

5 Is the head office in Massachussetts? _____

6 Does it have a factory in France? _____

7 Does it have retail stores in other countries? _____

8 Does Eileen work at the head office? _____

Countries

Write the missing letters in these country names.

1 BRA__IL   2 CANA__A   3 E__YPT   4 FR__NCE   5 RUS__IA   6 TH__ILAND

Cities

1 Match the cities and countries.

1 Auckland   ___ Argentina

2 Berlin   ___ China

3 Buenos Aires   ___ Germany

4 New Delhi   ___ India

5 Shanghai   ___ Italy

6 Venice   _1_ New Zealand

2 Write sentences about three of the cities.

Example   *Auckland is in New Zealand.*

_____

_____

_____

MODULE 4.5

Nationalities

1 Write the correct nationality for each company. Use these nationalities:

American	Chinese	French	Japanese	~~Korean~~	Swedish

1 Hyundai   <u>Korean</u>   4 Panasonic   _____
2 Ikea   _____   5 Peugeot   _____
3 Lenovo   _____   6 Starbucks   _____

2 Write sentences about three of the companies.

Example   *Hyundai is a Korean company.*

_____

_____

_____

MODULE 4.6

Company information

Write the words in each question in the correct order.

1 do   company   you   Which   for   work   ?
   <u>Which company do you work for?</u>

2 company   is   What   your   nationality   ?

_____

3 office   is   Where   head   the   ?

_____

4 does   have   it   Where   factories   ?

_____

5 work   you   do   Where   ?

_____

MODULE 4.7

A presentation

In your notebook, write about your company or a company you know. You can answer the questions in Module 4.6 and use the text in Module 4.2 as a model.

MODULE 4.8

1 Write the numbers in words. Use the words below.

four hundred	eight hundred fifty-eight
~~two hundred one~~	six hundred fifteen

1 201 <u>two hundred one</u>

2 400 _____

3 615 _____

4 858 _____

2 Now write these numbers in words.

1 110 _____

2 362 _____

3 537 _____

4 740 _____

5 990 _____

MODULE 4.9

Street addresses

1 Look at this.

The street address is Bose Corporation, The Mountain, Framingham, Massachussetts. That's M-A, zero one seven zero one dash nine one six eight, U-S-A.

Bose Corporation
The Mountain
Framingham, MA 01701-9168
USA

2 Write these addresses in the same way.

1 The street address is Bajaj Auto Ltd., Akurdi, Pune four one one zero three five, India.

_____
_____
_____
_____

2 The street address is Rip Curl, one oh one Surfcoast Highway, Torquay, Victoria. That's V-I-C, three two two eight, Australia.

_____
_____
_____
_____

MODULE 4.10

On the phone – Sorry, what was that?

Ted McKenzie is going to Vera Anderson's office in Boston. He calls to check her address. Number the lines of the conversation in the correct order.

Vera	*No, it's 723 Beacon Street.*	☐
Vera	*7-2-3 Beacon Street.*	☐
Ted	*I'm at the subway station. Is your address 733 Beacon Street?*	☐
Ted	*723. Fine. See you soon. Bye.*	☐
Vera	*Bye.*	☐
Vera	*Hi, Ted. Where are you?*	☐
Ted	*Hi, Vera. This is Ted.*	☐ 1
Ted	*Sorry, what was that?*	☐

MODULE 4.11

Culture corner – National products

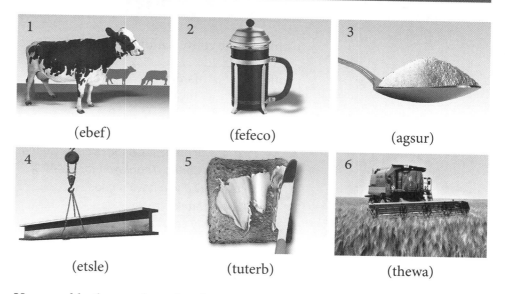

1 (ebef)

2 (fefeco)

3 (agsur)

4 (etsle)

5 (tuterb)

6 (thewa)

1 Unscramble the words under the pictures and complete the sentences.

1 Argentina produces <u>beef</u>.

2 Brazil produces _____.

3 Cuba produces _____.

4 China produces _____.

5 New Zealand produces _____.

6 The United States produces _____.

2 Write two similar sentences about your own country and one foreign country.

_____

_____

_____

_____

5

Meeting people

MODULE 5.1

Complete the conversations. Use the words below.

coffee	family	flight	~~meeting~~	parking
things	this	How	Which	

At the arrival lounge at the airport

A *Mr. Picard? My name is Chang. Dennis Chang.*

B *Ah, hello, Mr. Chang. Thank you for __meeting__ ¹ me.*

A *My pleasure. Did you have a good _____²?*

B *Pretty good, thanks.*

A *OK, let's go. My car is in the _____³ lot.*

In the elevator

A *Good afternoon, Ms. Lee.*

B *Oh, hello, Mr. Marques. _____⁴ floor?*

A *Fifth floor, please. _____⁵ are you today?*

B *Fine, thank you. And you?*

A *Pretty good, thank you. … Ah, _____⁶ is my floor.*

In the company restaurant

A *Jim, great to see you. How are _____⁷?*

B *Hey, Kazuo! Pretty good, thanks. How are the kids?*

A *Fine, thanks. And your _____⁸?*

B *Everyone's fine. How about a _____⁹?*

A *Good idea.*

MODULE 5.2   Greeting people

Write three conversations. Use the lines below.

Yeah, it's been ages!	~~Hello, I'm Karen Greenberg.~~
Pretty good, thank you. And you?	Hey, Joe, long time, no see!
Good to meet you, Ms. Greenberg.	Hello, Ms. Davis. How are you this morning?

Conversation 1 (Strangers)

A   _Hello, I'm Karen Greenberg._

B _____

Conversation 2 (Acquaintances)

A _____

B _____

Conversation 3 (Friends)

A _____

B _____

MODULE 5.3   Meet and greet

1   Look at the business card and text.

"Hi, my name's Dan Gunderson. I'm with MHC. I'm in the Public Relations Department. My office number is 312-544-2002."

2   Write your own card. Then write about yourself.

_____

_____

_____

_____

MODULE 5.4 — Introducing people

Look at the picture and read the conversation. Complete the information about the two people.

A *Ms. Nyman, I'd like you to meet Edward Oboya from the Export Department. Edward, this is Jennifer Nyman, from Nokia. Jennifer's in the Marketing Department.*

B *Hello, Ms. Nyman. Pleased to meet you.*

C *Hello, Mr. Oboya. Nice to meet you, too. Please call me Jenny.*

B *OK, Jenny. And I'm Eddie.*

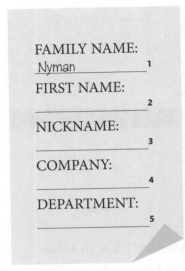

FAMILY NAME:
Nyman   **1**

FIRST NAME:
_____ **2**

NICKNAME:
_____ **3**

COMPANY:
_____ **4**

DEPARTMENT:
_____ **5**

FAMILY NAME:
Oboya   **6**

FIRST NAME:
_____ **7**

NICKNAME:
_____ **8**

COMPANY:
_____ **9**

DEPARTMENT:
_____ **10**

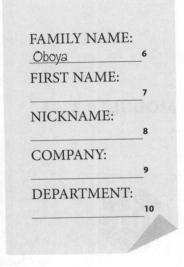

MODULE 5.5 — At the airport

Eriko Okada and her colleague, Kenji Wada, are at Osaka Airport to meet a customer from Serbia. Complete the conversation. Use the lines below.

Pretty good, thanks.	Nice to meet you, Ms. Okada.	No, thanks, I can manage.
Not at all.	Good to meet you, Mr. Wada.	~~Yes, that's right.~~

A *Ms. Anna Vidic?*

B Yes, that's right.   **1**

A *My name is Eriko Okada.*

B _____ **2**

A *Did you have a good flight?*

B _____ **3**

Thank you for meeting me.   **4**

A *I'd like you to meet my colleague, Kenji Wada.*   **5**

B _____

C *Pleased to meet you, too, Ms. Vidic. Can I give you a hand with your bags?*   **6**

B _____

Flight information

Air New Zealand flight NZ one zero to Honolulu is now boarding at gate fifteen.

Singapore Airlines flight SQ two eight six to Singapore is now boarding at gate eight.

Qantas flight AF one one four to Sydney is now boarding at gate eleven.

Emirates flight EK four three five to Dubai is now boarding at gate twelve.

This is the last call for Pacific Blue flight DJ one six three to Raratonga. Please go to gate five immediately.

1 Read the airport flight announcements above and complete the chart.

Airline	Flight no.	Destination	Gate	Remarks
Air New Zealand	NZ 10	Honolulu	15	boarding

2 Read the dialogue. Then write a similar dialogue about another flight in the chart, or use your own ideas.

A *Excuse me, what's the number of the Air New Zealand flight to Honolulu?*
B *NZ 10.*
A *Thank you. And what's the gate number?*
B *Gate 15.*
A *Thank you very much.*
B *You're welcome.*

A _____

_____

B _____
A _____
B _____
A _____
B _____

MODULE 5.7

Julia Chang is in San Francisco. She calls Brian Ellis, a business acquaintance in London. Number the lines of the conversation in the correct order.

Brian   *11:05. That's great. Which terminal?* ☐

Julia   *Yes, I think so. 0190-320-9157.* ☐

Brian   *VS 020. OK, see you at the arrivals gate. Do you have my
            mobile number? ☐

Brian   *That's it. See you tomorrow. Have a good flight!* ☐

Julia   *Hi, Brian. I'm calling about my flight from San Francisco.
            I arrive at Heathrow at 11:05 a.m. tomorrow.* ☐1

Brian   *Terminal 3. Right. What's the flight number?* ☐

Julia   *Terminal 3.* ☐

Julia   *VS 020. That's Virgin Atlantic.* ☐

*mobile number (British English) = cell phone number (American English)

MODULE 5.8

Culture corner – Shaking hands

1   Match the words and phrases with the pictures.

a   b   c

d   e   f

1 shake hands   ☐   4 air kiss   ☐

2 bow   ☐   5 kiss   ☐

3 hug   ☐   6 exchange business cards   ☐

2   Read this sentence about body language in business greetings in the United States.

In the United States, businesspeople usually shake hands when they meet.

Write a similar sentence about your own country.

_____

_____

In the office

MODULE 6.1

Could I use your calculator?

1 Complete these office conversations. Use the words below.

ahead	any	borrow	~~for~~	lot
on	minute	problem	run	

Conversation 1

A *Could I use your eraser* <u>for</u> ¹ *a minute?*

B *Uh, yeah, go* _____². *It's in that drawer.*

A *Thanks a* _____³.

Conversation 2

A *Could I* _____⁴ *your calculator, Dave?*

B *Yes, sure. It's* _____⁵ *the shelf.*

A *Terrific. I'll bring it back in a* _____⁶.

Conversation 3

A *Could I use your staples? I've* _____⁷ *out.*

B *Sorry, I don't have* _____⁸.

A *No* _____⁹. *Thanks anyway.*

2 Write a similar conversation. Use your own ideas.

A _____

B _____

A _____

B _____

Things in the office

Write the names of the things in the puzzle. After you finish, read down to find the mystery word.

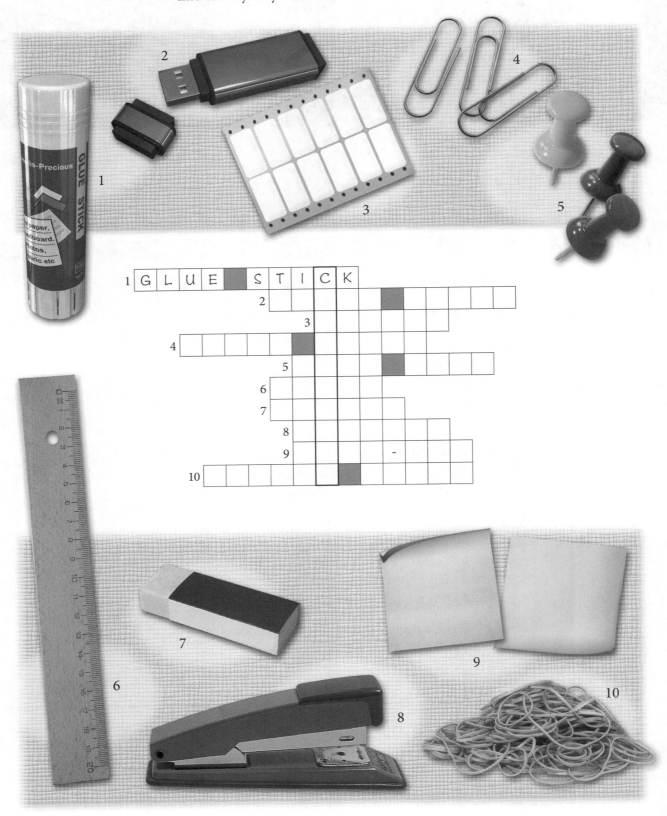

1 G L U E ▨ S T I C K

1   Match the words with the items (1–12) in the picture.

apple   8   laptop   ☐

books   ☐   notepad   ☐

briefcase   ☐   pen   ☐

calendar   ☐   phone   ☐

camera   ☐   photographs   ☐

coffee cup   ☐   plant   ☐

keys   ☐   sandwich   ☐

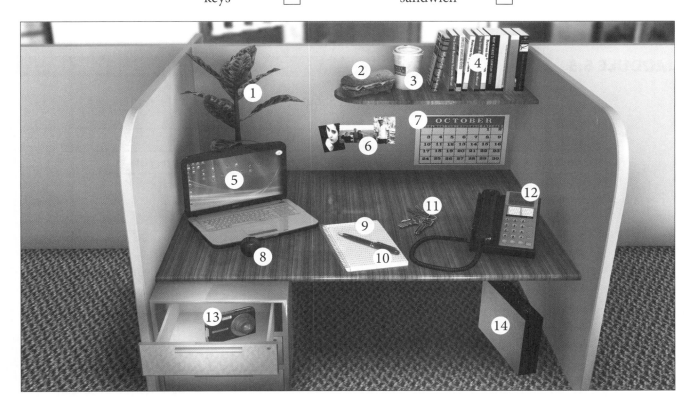

2   Look at the picture in Exercise 1. Circle ◯ *T* (true) or *F* (false) for each sentence.

1	There's a briefcase on the desk.	T	(F)
2	There are some keys between the phone and the notepad.	T	F
3	There's a plant in front of the laptop.	T	F
4	There are some photographs on the partition.	T	F
5	There's a camera in the drawer.	T	F
6	There's a sandwich next to the coffee cup.	T	F
7	There are some books below the calendar.	T	F

3   Correct the false sentences and write them below.

1 There's a briefcase under the desk.

_____

_____

MODULE 6.4   Electronics

Read the conversation below. Write a similar conversation about an electronic item you have. You are Speaker B.

A That's a nice <u>camera</u>.
(MP3 player / cell phone, etc.)
B Thanks.
A What make is it?
B It's <u>a Nikon</u>.
(a Canon / Leica, etc.)
A Are you happy with it?
B Yes, I am. It's <u>excellent</u>.
(very good / great, etc.)

A _____
B _____
A _____
B _____
A _____
B _____

MODULE 6.5   Netbooks

1 Look at the information about a netbook and read the sentences.

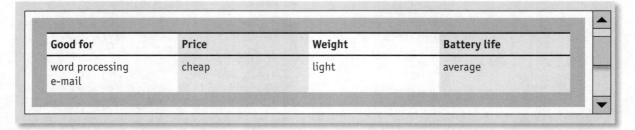

Good for	Price	Weight	Battery life
word processing e-mail	cheap	light	average

This model is good for word processing and e-mail. It's cheap, light, and battery life is average.

2 Use this information to write similar sentences.

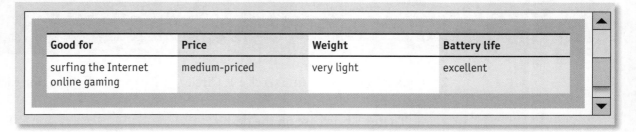

Good for	Price	Weight	Battery life
surfing the Internet online gaming	medium-priced	very light	excellent

This model _____

_____

3 Write about a netbook you would like to buy. Use your own ideas.

This model _____

_____

MODULE 6.6

An electronics store

Complete the conversation in an electronics store. Use the words below.

bit	for	is	much	not	one	am	think	very

A *Are you looking _____¹ a camera, ma'am?*
B *Yes, I _____².*
A *This _____³ is very popular. It's a Nikon.*
B *How _____⁴ is it?*
A *$499.*
B *That's a _____⁵ expensive.*
A *Well, it's _____⁶ small, and the lens _____⁷ excellent.*
B *Mm. I'm _____⁸ sure. I need to _____⁹ about it.*

MODULE 6.7

On the phone – Sure, no problem

Sophie Milne calls her colleague, Nazri Amar. Number the lines of the conversation in the correct order.

Sophie *Hi, Nazri. It's Sophie Milne.* ☐

Sophie *Five o'clock is fine. See you then. Bye.* ☐

Nazri *Tomorrow morning? Sure, no problem.* ☐

Nazri *Nazri Amar speaking.* ☐ 1

Sophie *Could I use your laptop tomorrow morning?*
It's for my presentation. ☐

Nazri *Hi, Sophie. What can I do for you?* ☐

Nazri *Bye.* ☐

Nazri *Sorry, I'm a little busy right now. Is five o'clock OK?* ☐

Sophie *Great, thanks. Can I pick it up now?* ☐

MODULE 6.8

Culture corner – Is your desk a mess?

1 Match the sentence halves.

1 If you don't need something today,
2 Don't have more than
3 Don't eat or
4 Clear your desk
5 Don't have a
6 Keep rulers, erasers, etc.

___ in a desk drawer.
___ plant on your desk.
___ at the end of the day.
___ drink at your desk.
___ three pens on your desk.
_1_ file it, or shred it.

2 Write advice about keeping your desk neat. Use one of the ideas above, or your own idea.

Example   *If you don't need something today, file it, or shred it.*

Work

MODULE 7.1

Jobs

Four people talk about their jobs. Complete the information. Use the words below.

a	an	design	for	help	large
manager	~~my~~	near	run	work	visit

Hi, _my_ ¹ name's Lise Pedersen. I'm _____ ² designer. I work for a large cell phone company. I _____ ³ cell phones.

Hello, I'm Stephen Schroder. I'm a sales _____ ⁴. I work for a _____ ⁵ wine company in South Africa. I _____ ⁶ customers all over the world.

Hello, I'm Laya Patel. I'm a ground hostess. I work _____ ⁷ Air India. I _____ ⁸ passengers at Indira Gandhi International Airport, _____ ⁹ New Delhi.

Hi, My name's Takashi Ishida. I'm _____ ¹⁰ engineer. I _____ ¹¹ for a major Formula 1 team. I _____ ¹² the Engineering Department.

Complete the crossword puzzle.

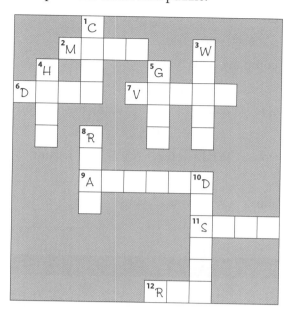

Across

2 Do you ___ photocopies for the files?

6 We ___ with complaints from customers.

7 I ___ customers in the Tokyo area.

9 We ___ a lot of meetings.

11 I ___ insurance to customers.

12 I ___ the Publicity Department.

Down

1 I ___ customers every day.

3 Do you ___ many e-mails?

4 We ___ customers if they have problems.

5 I often ___ presentations at trade fairs and conferences.

8 Do you ___ many reports?

10 I ___ buildings. I really enjoy it.

MODULE 7.3

Jobs and duties

Write the words in each question in the correct order.

1 do   What   do   you   ?
   What do you do?

2 company   Which   you   do   for   work   ?
   _____

3 is   What   of   it   company   kind   ?
   _____

4 you   What   do   in   job   your   do   ?
   _____

5 job   Do   you   your   like   ?
   _____

MODULE 7.4

Your job

1 Look at the information and read the text below.

Name	Marina Kovacs
Job	website designer
Company	JK Design
Kind of company	design agency
Location	Hong Kong
Duties	run the Web Design Department, design corporate websites

"My name's Marina Kovacs. I'm a website designer. I work for JK Design, a design agency in Hong Kong. I run the Web Design Department, and I design corporate websites. My job is great."

2 Complete the information about you.

Name	
Job	
Company	
Kind of company	
Location	
Duties	

3 Write sentences about you and your job. Use the information above.

_____

_____

MODULE 7.5

Read the e-mail and answer the questions. Write short answers.

✉ **E-mail**

Date: Tuesday, November 23, 2010 4:42 p.m.
From: Margaret Rainer <mrainer@ntjp.com>
To: Gavin Benson <gabenson@ntjp.com>
Subject: Project meeting

Gavin,

Could you get everything ready for the project meeting tomorrow?

• e-mail everyone about the time and place (3:00 p.m., Room 409)

• make twelve copies of the agenda

• check the PowerPoint slides

• set up the projector

Thanks.

Best wishes,
Maggie

---

1 Who is the e-mail from?   _Margaret Rainer_

2 Who is it to?   _____

3 What is it about?   _____

4 What time is the meeting?   _____

5 Where is it?   _____

6 How many copies of the agenda does she want?   _____

7 What does she want Gavin to check?   _____

8 What does she want him to set up?   _____

MODULE 7.6

Cross out the words which don't match the words on the right.

1 turn on / turn off / ~~shred~~   the air conditioner
2 copy / unlock / check   the price list
3 print / call / write to   Mr. Chang
4 copy / close / open   the door
5 install / delete / call   the software
6 shred / copy / turn off   the documents
7 recycle / turn on / read   the newspapers

MODULE 7.7　　　On the phone – Please ask him to call me

Takashi Kondo is calling Dorothy Brewster. He speaks to Anne Chung.
Number the lines of the conversation in the correct order.

Takashi	*Could I leave a message?*	☐
Anne	*090-5551-7241. I'll give her your message.*	☐
Anne	*I'm afraid she's not here at the moment.*	☐
Anne	*Goodbye.*	☐
Takashi	*Please ask her to call my cell phone number.* *It's 090-5551-7241.*	☐
Takashi	*Thank you. Goodbye.*	☐
Takashi	*Hello, this is Takashi Kondo of Nissan. Could I speak to* *Ms. Brewster in the Publicity Department, please?*	1
Anne	*Yes, of course.*	☐

MODULE 7.8　　　Culture corner – Men or women?

1 Are these statements true or false? Circle ◯ T or F for each one. Then check
your answers on page 69.

1	In New York, taxi drivers are usually women.	**T**	**F**
2	In Vietnam, most agricultural workers are women.	**T**	**F**
3	In the United States, nurses are usually men.	**T**	**F**
4	In China, scientists and technicians are usually men.	**T**	**F**
5	In the UK, primary school teachers are usually women.	**T**	**F**
6	In Asia, politicians are usually women.	**T**	**F**

2 Write two sentences about jobs in your country, city, or area.

In my country, _____

_____

_____

_____

8

Appointments

MODULE 8.1

Two meetings

1   Complete the phone conversation. Use the words below.

about	do	good	meet	on
~~speaking~~	then	time	want	your

A *Hello, Mr. Viera? Paul O'Connor _speaking_ ¹.*

B *Oh, hello, Mr. O'Connor. What can I _____² for you?*

A *I _____³ to talk about the new website design. Can we _____⁴ on September the 15th?*

B *Just a moment, let me check. What _____⁵?*

A *How _____⁶ the morning, at ten o'clock?*

B *Yes, ten o'clock is _____⁷.*

A *Is _____⁸ office OK?*

B *Sure. See you _____⁹ the 15th.*

A *Yes, see you _____¹⁰. Bye.*

B *Bye.*

2   Read the phone conversation again. Answer the questions.

1   Who wants to have a meeting?   _____

2   What about?   _____

3   What date is it?   _____

4   What time is it?   _____

5   Where is it?   _____

MODULE 8.2

Find the months of the year in the word square.

A	S	O	V	M	A	R	C	H	O	C
A	U	J	Y	J	A	N	U	A	R	Y	A
P	A	U	G	U	S	T	Y	T	V	F	F
J	R	S	O	N	Y	C	S	O	J	E	N
O	B	E	M	E	A	U	G	A	R	B	O
Y	E	P	C	Y	V	E	R	P	Y	R	V
O	C	T	O	B	E	R	S	R	M	U	E
C	T	E	S	Y	M	A	C	I	A	A	M
V	J	M	R	S	B	J	U	L	Y	R	B
E	C	B	Y	F	E	A	J	M	O	Y	E
M	F	E	D	E	C	E	M	B	E	R	R
O	E	R	S	T	T	C	B	R	A	U	O

MODULE 8.3

Ordinal numbers

Write the ordinal numbers.

first	_1st_	second	_____
third	_____	fourth	_____
nineteenth	_____	twentieth	_____
twenty-first	_____	twenty-second	_____
thirtieth	_____	thirty-first	_____

MODULE 8.4

Dates

Write answers to the questions.

What's the date today?

It's _____

When's your birthday?

_____

What's an important date for you? Why?

_____

_____

_____

MODULE 8.5   Clock times

1   Write these times as digits.

1   one twenty   <u>1:20</u>   4   eight thirty-two   _____

2   six fifty-nine   _____   5   three ten   _____

3   five oh five   _____   6   nine forty   _____

2   Write these times in words.

1   4:40   <u>four forty</u>   4   10:05   _____

2   7:23   _____   5   12:35   _____

3   2:50   _____   6   9:25   _____

MODULE 8.6   Scheduling a meeting

1   Pete wants to schedule a meeting with a co-worker. Look at his notes and complete the phone conversation.

– meeting with Junko

– talk about advertising

– 18th (Tuesday), ~~2 p.m.~~ 10 a.m.

– Junko's office

A   Hi, <u>Junko</u>¹. It's Pete.

B   Hi, Pete, what can I do for you?

A   I want to talk about _____². Can we meet on Tuesday the _____³th?

B   What time?

A   How about _____⁴ p.m.?

B   Sorry, I'm busy then. How about _____⁵ a.m.?

A   Yes, that's fine. Is your _____⁶ OK?

B   Sure. See you then. Bye.

A   Bye.

2   You want to schedule a meeting with a co-worker. Write your notes (co-worker's name, meeting topic, date and time, place) below, then write a similar conversation.

Meeting with

_____

_____

_____

_____

_____

_____

1 Three people, Amy (A), Ben (B), and Chet (C), want to schedule a meeting.
Complete the conversation. Use the sentences below.

How about 10:30? How about 9 a.m.? ~~OK, let's start.~~ See you then!	
Well, how about the small meeting room? Yes, the 18th is fine with me.	

A <u>OK, let's start.</u>   ¹ *I want to schedule a meeting to talk about overtime. Is Friday the 18th OK?*

B _____ ²

C *The 18th is OK with me, too.*

A _____ ³

B *Yes, 9 a.m. is fine.*

C *Sorry, I'm busy then.* _____ ⁴

B *10:30? Yes, OK.*

A *OK, 10:30 a.m. Is the large meeting room OK?*

B _____ ⁵

A *The small meeting room? OK.*

C *Yes, the small room is better.*

A *OK, so that's Friday the 18th at 10:30.* _____ ⁶

2 After the meeting Amy writes an e-mail to Ben and Chet. There are three
mistakes in her information. Circle ◯ them.

✉ **E-mail message**

Date:	Monday, February 14, 2011 10:31 a.m.
From:	Amy Chen <achen@tswebsoft.com>
To:	Ben Oaks <benoaks@tswebsoft.com, chetdavis@tswebsoft.com>
Subject:	Meeting

Dear Ben and Chet,

It was good to talk to you today. Here are the details of the meeting:
topic – overtime
date – Friday the ⟨19th⟩
time – 9 a.m.
place – large meeting room

See you there!

Best wishes,

Amy

3 Correct the information like this:

1 <u>The meeting isn't on Friday the 19th, it's on Friday the 18th.</u>

2 _____

   _____

3 _____

   _____

MODULE 8.8

John Woo calls his co-worker, Mark White. Number the lines of the conversation in the correct order.

John	*Terrific. I'm really sorry about that.*	☐
Mark	*That's too bad.*	☐
John	*It's about our meeting this afternoon. I'm afraid I can't make it. Something's come up.*	☐
John	*Hi, Mark. It's John.*	1
Mark	*Don't worry about it. Bye.*	☐
Mark	*Hang on, I'll check. … Yes, tomorrow is fine.*	☐
John	*Bye.*	☐
Mark	*Hi, John. What can I do for you?*	☐
John	*Can we make it tomorrow, same time?*	☐

MODULE 8.9

1 Read the information.

Bastille Day is a special day in France. It's on July 14th. Families meet and have a large meal. There are a lot of fireworks and parades.

Thanksgiving is a special day in the United States. It's on the fourth Thursday in November. Families and friends get together and have a large meal. Many people watch football on TV.

Vesak is a special day in some Asian countries such as India and Thailand. It's in May or June. It's a Buddhist holiday. Many people visit temples, wear special clothes, and eat only vegetarian food.

2 Write similar information about a special day in your country, or a country you know.

_____

_____

_____

_____

9

Directions and shopping

MODULE 9.1

The city center

Complete the conversations. Use the words below.

and	Excuse	from	me	near	of	~~there~~	to

1 **A** *Excuse me, is* <u>there</u> *a health club near here?*
   B *Yes, there's one on Birch Street, next _____ the station.*
2 **A** *Pardon me, is there a car rental place _____ here?*
   B *Sure, there's one on Oak Street, between the post office _____
       the gas station.*
3 **A** *_____ me, is there a coffee shop near here?*
   B *Yes, there's one on Elm Street, across _____ the park.*
4 **A** *Pardon _____, is there a subway station near here?*
   B *Yes, there's one on the corner _____ Oak Street and Eleventh Street.*

MODULE 9.2

Directions

Match the sentences with the maps.

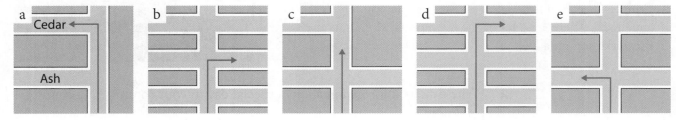

1 Go along this street. `c`
2 Turn left at the first intersection.
3 Turn right at the second intersection.
4 Go along this street and turn left onto Cedar Street.
5 Go along this street and turn right at the third intersection.

MODULE 9.3

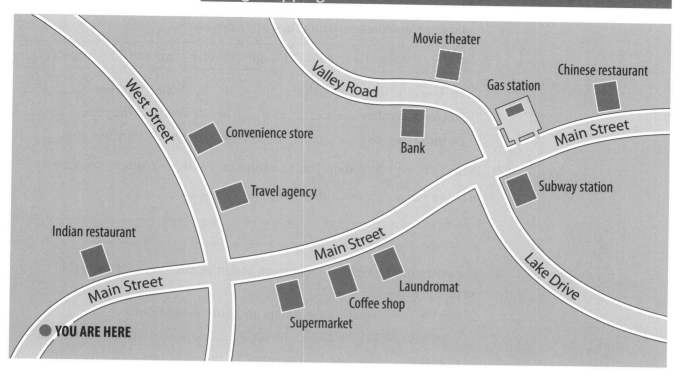

1 Look at the map and read the conversation.

A *Excuse me, is there a convenience store near here?*

B *Yes, there's one on West Street. Go along this street. Turn left at the first intersection. It's on the right, near the travel agency.*

2 Write two more conversations about other places on the map.

_____

_____

_____

_____

_____

_____

_____

_____

MODULE 9.4

Numbers 1,000–1,000,000

Write the numbers in words.

1 2,000 _two thousand_ _____

2 4,540 _____

3 11,280 _____

4 429,600 _____

5 987,018 _____

MODULE 9.5

1 Complete the sentences using the currencies below.

| baht (B) | ~~dollars~~ ($) | euros (€) | pesos (MX$) | pounds (£) | rupees (₹) |

1 In Australia they use <u>dollars</u>. 4 In Mexico they use _____.

2 In Germany they use _____. 5 In Thailand they use _____.

3 In India they use _____. 6 In the UK they use _____.

2 Write two sentences about your country and another country you know.

In ... we use ... . In ... they use ... .

_____

_____

3 The prices on the right are incorrect. Find the mistakes and write the correct prices.

1 $99.99   Ninety-nine dollars and ninety-~~eight~~ ^{nine} cents
<u>Ninety-nine dollars and ninety-nine cents</u>

2 ¥126,000   One hundred twenty-five thousand yen
_____

3 ₩24,000   Thirty-four thousand won
_____

4 B520   Five hundred twelve baht
_____

MODULE 9.6

Write the words in each sentence in the correct order.

1 bottle for I'm a looking perfume of
<u>I'm looking for a bottle of perfume.</u>

2 a my for wife It's gift
_____

3 expensive little a That's
_____

4 it you gift-wrapped like Would ?
_____

5 would How you pay to like ?
_____

6 you Visa Do take ?
_____

MODULE 9.7 — Buying a gift

1 Eric Reid is in the shopping area at Heathrow Airport. Read the conversation.

A *Good afternoon. Can I help you?*
B *Yes, I'm looking for a watch. It's a gift for my daughter.*
A *I see. How about this one?*
B *How much is it?*
A *It's $289.*
B *That's a little expensive. How much is that one?*
A *It's $99.*
B *Yes, that's fine. I'll take it.*
A *Fine. Would you like it gift-wrapped?*
B *No, thank you.*
A *How would you like to pay?*
B *By credit card. Do you take American Express?*
A *Yes, of course.*

2 Write answers to the questions. Use the answers below.

Yes, it is.	By credit card.	~~A watch.~~	No, it's for his daughter.
Yes, they do.	No, he doesn't.	Yes, he does.	No, it's a little expensive.

1 What is he looking for?
   A watch.
   _____

2 Is it a gift for his wife?
   _____

3 Is $289 OK?
   _____

4 Is $99 OK?
   _____

5 Does he buy it?
   _____

6 Does he want it gift-wrapped?
   _____

7 How does he pay?
   _____

8 Do they take American Express?
   _____

MODULE 9.8   On the phone – Can I have your credit card number?

Carmen Garcia calls a florist to order some flowers. Number the lines of the conversation in the correct order.

Florist   *Certainly. Large or small?* ☐

Florist   *June 2018. Thank you. And just one more thing. The security number on the back?* ☐

Florist   *Good morning, Mandy's Flowers. May I help you?* ☐ 1

Carmen   *Small, please.* ☐

Carmen   *Yes, just a moment. It's 4591753662. And the expiration date* is June 2018.* ☐

Florist   *446. Thank you.* ☐

Florist   *One small lily bouquet. Can I have your credit card number, please, Ms. Garcia?* ☐

Carmen   *Yes, my name is Garcia. I'd like to order a lily bouquet for a birthday.* ☐

Carmen   *The security number? Er … 446.* ☐

*expiration date = you can use your card up to this date

MODULE 9.9   Culture corner – Cash or card?

1   Unscramble the words.

1   shac   cash
2   ibdte acdr _____
3   inrat rdca _____

4   rdteci drac _____
5   yalPaP _____
6   ecckh _____

2   Gino Franzetti is an Italian businessperson. How does he pay for things? Read what he says.

> I use cash at my local coffee shop. I pay by debit card at the supermarket. I don't use my credit card for Internet shopping – I use PayPal.

How do you pay for things? Write two or three sentences about yourself.

I use / pay by … .   *I don't use / pay by … .*

_____

_____

_____

_____

10

Reservations

MODULE 10.1

Making a reservation

Complete the conversations. Use the words below.

| double | from | like | many | May | or |
| quiet | ~~reserve~~ | room | see | time | Which |

Conversation 1

A *Can I help you?*

B *Yes, I'd like to <u>reserve</u> ¹ a car for three days.*

A *_____² class would you like?*

B *Compact.*

A *Manual _____³ automatic?*

B *Automatic, please.*

A *Yes, that's OK. May I _____⁴ your driver's license, please?*

Conversation 2

A *Star of India Restaurant. May I help you?*

B *Yes, I'd _____⁵ to reserve a table for two for this evening.*

A *Certainly, sir. For what _____⁶?*

B *8:30. And I'd like a _____⁷ table, please.*

A *Yes, of course. Could I have your name, please?*

Conversation 3

A *Station Hotel. May I help you?*

B *Yes, I'd like to reserve a _____⁸.*

A *Certainly. For how _____⁹ nights?*

B *For four nights, _____¹⁰ August 21st to 25th.*

A *Single or _____¹¹?*

B *Single, please.*

A *Yes, that's fine. _____¹² I have your name, please?*

1   Look at the information and complete the phone conversation.

Milano			
Number of people	**Time**	**Name**	**Special requests**
4	8:00 p.m.	Larsen	table near the window

A Good afternoon, <u>Milano</u> ¹ Restaurant. May I help you?
B Yes, I'd like to reserve a table for _____² for this evening.
A Certainly, madam. For what time?
B _____³ o'clock.
A Yes, that's fine. May I have your name, please?
B _____⁴. And I'd like a table _____⁵ the window, please.
A Yes, that's fine, Ms. Larsen.

2   Match the tables in the picture with the phrases.

1 a corner table	☐	3 a table near the window	☐
2 a table near the stage	☐	4 a table on the terrace	☐

3   Write the information for your reservation. Use your own name and your own ideas.

Sevilla			
Number of people	**Time**	**Name**	**Special requests**

4   Use the information to write a similar phone conversation.

A _____
B _____
A _____
B _____
A _____
B _____
A _____

MODULE 10.3   Reserving a flight

1 Match the questions with the answers.

1	How may I help you?	___ From Paris.
2	Where from?	___ Business.
3	Where to?	___ September 5th.
4	When would you like to depart?	_1_ I'd like to make a flight reservation.
5	When would you like to return?	___ Seoul.
6	How many passengers?	___ September 9th.
7	Which flight class?	___ Just one.

2 Answer the questions above, using your own ideas.

1 I'd like to make a flight reservation. _____

2 _____

3 _____

4 _____

5 _____

6 _____

7 _____

MODULE 10.4   Time periods

Write about each hotel reservation.

1 September 25th, 26th
   September 25th and 26th. That's two nights. _____

2 May 10th–14th

   _____

3 July 2nd–8th

   _____

4 August 12th–16th

   _____

5 October 10th, 11th

   _____

MODULE 10.5 — Making a hotel reservation

Read the e-mail. Answer the questions. Use short answers.

✉ E-mail message

To: The Cohasset Inn
Subject: Reservation

I'd like to reserve a single room – at your Internet price of $120 per night – for three nights, from June 14th to 17th. I would like a quiet, non-smoking room, please.

I look forward to hearing from you.

Sarah Cohen

---

1 Who is the e-mail from? _____

2 What is it about? _____

3 Does she want a double room? _____

4 How much is it per night? _____

5 How many nights does she want to stay? _____

6 Does she have any special requests? _____

MODULE 10.6 — Renting a car

1 Write the missing words in the information. Use the words and phrases below.

| air conditioning | automatic | Economy | GPS | Premium |

ProChoice Vehicle Rental

Type of car: ☐ Mini ☐ _____ ¹
☐ Compact ☐ _____ ²
☐ manual ☐ _____ ³

Options: ☐ a child seat ☐ _____ ⁴ ☐ _____ ⁵

2 Read the text, then write your own. You can use your own ideas if you like.

"I'd like to reserve a Mini class car with manual transmission. I'd like a child seat and GPS."

_____

_____

_____

MODULE 10.7

Michel Picard calls a restaurant and speaks to the manager. Number the lines of the conversation in the correct order.

Michel	*That's right. I'd like to change it to eight o'clock, if possible.*	☐
Manager	*Just one moment, Mr. Picard. May I have your first name, please?*	☐
Manager	*Good morning. Thai Garden restaurant. How may I help you?*	1
Michel	*Thank you very much. Goodbye.*	☐
Manager	*Let me see. Yes, that's fine. So that's a table for two at eight o'clock. We look forward to seeing you this evening.*	☐
Manager	*Goodbye.*	☐
Michel	*Good morning. My name is Picard. I have a reservation for this evening.*	☐
Manager	*Ah yes, Mr. Michel Picard. That's a table for two at 8:30.*	☐
Michel	*Michel.*	☐

MODULE 10.8

Culture corner – A place to stay

1 George Baker is an American businessperson. He is planning a business trip to Osaka. Read the message.

✉ **E-mail message**

I'm going to Osaka next month. I want to stay at a small, friendly hotel. I'm looking for a place with Internet access and an exercise room. A convenient location is important.

2 You are planning a business trip to a foreign city. Choose the city and write a similar message.

✉ **E-mail message**

_____

_____

_____

_____

_____

Requests and offers

MODULE 11.1

In the office

Complete the conversations. Use the words below.

about	anyway	busy	course	install	later
~~open~~	right	Sure	tell	Thank	Thanks

Conversation 1

A Could you _open_ ¹ the door for me?

B Yes, of _____².

A Great. _____³ you.

Conversation 2

A Could you _____⁴ me your new cell phone number?

B _____⁵, it's 735-555-7269.

A _____⁶.

Conversation 3

A Could you _____⁷ the new spreadsheet software for me?

B Sorry, I don't have time _____⁸ now. Could you ask Monica?

A OK. Thanks _____⁹.

Conversation 4

A Could you e-mail Mr. Park _____¹⁰ the sales figures?

B Sorry, I'm _____¹¹ right now.

A OK. Could you do it _____¹²?

B Yes, sure.

Complete the crossword puzzle.

Across

Could you …

3 _____ on the light? It's getting dark.

6 _____ off the air conditioner? It's cold in here.

7 _____ these packages today?

8 _____ the door? I want to talk to you in private.

11 _____ the phone for me?

12 _____ some coffee for the meeting?

Down

Could you …

1 _____ me a sandwich from the cafeteria?

2 _____ this software for me? I can't do it.

4 _____ this printer cartridge? It's empty.

5 _____ to Ms. Lee about her visit?

9 _____ the safe? I can't remember the combination.

10 _____ these figures? I think there's a mistake.

MODULE 11.3 Could you …?

A boss is speaking to an employee. Write the lines of the conversation in the correct order.

Sorry, I'm giving a presentation this afternoon.   Yes, of course.
Ah, yes. Well, could you do it tomorrow morning?   Thanks.
Could you check the new website this afternoon?

A _____

B _____

A _____

B _____

A _____

MODULE 11.4 Deadlines

Read the e-mail from a web designer to his assistant. Answer the questions. Write short answers.

✉ **E-mail message**

Date: Wednesday, July 13, 2011 2:06 PM
From: Jerry Weiss <jweiss@wkd.com>
To: Vince Fox <vjfox@wkd.com>
Subject: Westech website

Vince,

Re. the website for Westech Engineering. Could you choose the photographs by tomorrow morning? Also, could you check the text? I think there are some typos*. Could you do that by tomorrow evening? Sorry to rush you, but we don't have much time – as you know, it goes online Monday.

Thanks for all the hard work!

Jerry

---

*typo = a mistake in a text (typographical error)

1 Who is the message from? _____

2 Who is it to? _____

3 What is it about? _____

4 What does Jerry want Vince to choose? _____

5 What is the deadline? _____

6 What does Jerry want Vince to check? _____

7 When by? _____

8 When does the website go online? _____

MODULE 11.5

Write an offer for each situation. Use the ideas below and / or your own ideas.

| call the repair person | call you a taxi | get some sandwiches |
| open the window | ~~set up the projector~~ | recycle the newspapers |

1 Your boss is giving a presentation later today.

   Should I set up the projector?

2 The air conditioner is broken.

3 Your boss wants to get to the station in a hurry.

4 You and your colleagues don't have time for lunch in the cafeteria.

5 There are a lot of old newspapers on the desk.

6 It's very hot in the office.

MODULE 11.6

A class party

Write about plans for a real or imaginary class party. Write the day, date, time, and location. Also, write about what two or three people are doing at the party.

Example:

Our class party is on Wednesday, September 14th at 5:00 p.m. in this room.
Ms. Kim is choosing the music, and Mr. Kennedy is playing the guitar.
Mr. Watanabe is making a short speech.

On the phone – I just remembered

Jack Ellis is out of the office. He calls his colleague, Akira Nomura. Number the lines of the conversation in the correct order.

Jack	*Oh, terrific. Thanks very much. I appreciate it.*	☐
Jack	*Listen, could you check my computer?*	☐
Akira	*Just a moment, I'll take a look. … No, it's OK, it's off.*	☐
Jack	*Akira? It's Jack.*	1
Akira	*No problem. Bye.*	☐
Jack	*I think it's still on.*	☐
Akira	*Hi, Jack. What's up?*	☐
Akira	*Your computer? Sure. What's the problem?*	☐

MODULE 11.8

Culture corner – Who can you ask?

1 Complete the requests. Use the words in the box.

copy	discount	give	lend

1 Could you _____ this camera?

2 Could you _____ these documents for me?

3 Could you _____ me some money for the coffee machine?

4 Could you _____ me some advice about my presentation?

2 Write things you can ask two of the people below. Use the requests in Exercise 1 and / or your own ideas.

a senior co-worker	a co-worker and friend
a junior co-worker	a sales clerk

I think you can ask a senior co-worker "Could you give me some advice about my presentation?"

I think you can ask …

_____

_____

_____

_____

12

Socializing

MODULE 12.1

In a coffee shop

Complete the conversation in a coffee shop. Use the words below.

about	at	food	have	interesting	love
near	OK	something	sounds	think	~~would~~

A OK, Megumi. What <u>would</u>[1] you like to drink?

B A caffè latte, please.

A Would you like _____[2] to eat?

B No, thanks.

A Right. (to counter person) Excuse me? Two caffè lattes, please.

…

A So, what do you _____[3] of Boston, Megumi?

B It's great. Very _____[4].

A Good. Listen, would you like to _____[5] dinner Friday evening?

B Thank you. That would be great.

A Do you like Mexican _____[6]?

B Well, it's _____[7].

A How _____[8] Indian?

B Oh yes, I _____[9] Indian food.

A There's a good Indian restaurant _____[10] here.

B That _____[11] be great.

A We can meet _____[12] your hotel. Is 7:30 OK?

B Yes, that's fine.

At the counter

Write the words in each sentence in the correct order. Add punctuation and capital letters.

A *What would you like to drink?*
B *iced / please / coffee / an*

_____ 1

A *Would you like something to eat?*
B *chip / please / thanks / chocolate / yes / cookie / a*

_____ 2

A *OK. (to counter person) Excuse me?*
coffees / and / chip / a / please / cookie / chocolate / iced / two

_____
_____ 3

MODULE 12.3

Places

1 Write the letters of each word in the correct order.

1 z a g i n a m   <u>amazing</u>
2 c r i t i f e r   _____
3 n i c a f s t a t   _____
4 t a g r e   _____
5 d u l f r e w n o   _____
6 t e x g i n c i   _____

2 Read the example. Then write a question and answer about your town or city.

A *What do you think of Djakarta?*
B *It's really interesting.*

_____
_____

MODULE 12.4

Write the sentences below on the correct lines to make two conversations.

> How about the day after tomorrow?
> Yes, the 16th is fine. I'll look forward to it.
> What about a game next Sunday? That's the 16th.
> I'd love to, but tomorrow's a bit difficult.
> Thursday? Yes, that's good for me.
> I'd love to, but this Sunday is a bit difficult.

A *Would you like to play golf this Sunday?*

B _____ 1

A _____ 2

B _____ 3

A *Excellent.*

A *Would you like to have lunch tomorrow?*

B _____ 4

A _____ 5

B _____ 6

A *Great.*

MODULE 12.5

Food

1 Answer the questions. Use true information about you. You can use these answers:

> Yes, I love it.   Yes, I do.   Well, it's OK.
> No, I'm afraid I don't.   Actually, I haven't tried it.

1 Do you like Chinese food?

_____

2 Do you like Mexican food?

_____

3 Do you like Italian food?

_____

4 Do you like Turkish food?

_____

2 A business acquaintance (A) is asking you (B) about another kind of food. Write the question and answer.

A _____

B _____

MODULE 12.6 Restaurants

Read the example. Change the underlined words and write two similar conversations about restaurants you know.

A *There's a great Indian restaurant near the subway station.*
B *That sounds terrific.*

A _____

B _____

A _____

B _____

MODULE 12.7 Meeting up

Circle ◯ the correct underlined words in the conversation.

A *We do / can / are¹ meet in / on / to² the hotel lobby. Is 6:30 OK / well / right³?*
B *Could we do / meet / make⁴ it seven o'clock?*
A *Yes, seven o'clock are / is / be⁵ fine.*
B *Great. See you after / then / late⁶.*

MODULE 12.8 Role play

Look at the conversation in Module 12.1. Write a similar conversation between you and an American business acquaintance, Bob Mansell. You are at a coffee shop in your town or city. You are speaker A.

A _____

B _____

A _____

B _____

A _____

B _____

A _____

B _____

A _____

B _____

A _____

B _____

A _____

B _____

A _____

B _____

MODULE 12.9 | On the phone – Thank you very much for everything

Jung-Soo Kim is at Kennedy Airport after a business trip to the US. He calls Barbara Chavez at the New York office. Number the lines of the conversation in the correct order.

Barbara	*My pleasure. Have a good trip.*	☐
Jung-Soo	*Hello, Barbara? It's Jung-Soo.*	1
Jung-Soo	*Yes, I will. Ah, we're boarding. Thanks again, Barbara. Bye.*	☐
Jung-Soo	*Thanks. It'll be good to get home.*	☐
Barbara	*Bye.*	☐
Jung-Soo	*Yes, I'm at the departure gate. Thank you very much for everything.*	☐
Barbara	*Oh, hi, Jung-Soo. Are you at the airport?*	☐
Barbara	*And give my regards to everybody at the Seoul office.*	☐

MODULE 12.10 | Culture corner – Places to visit

1 Read Jim Halliday's e-mail to a co-worker, Salman Latif. Salman is going to visit Bangkok for the first time to make a presentation at a conference.

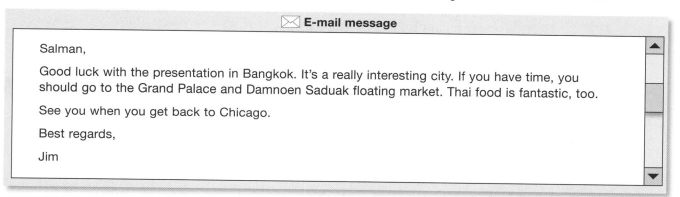

✉ **E-mail message**

Salman,

Good luck with the presentation in Bangkok. It's a really interesting city. If you have time, you should go to the Grand Palace and Damnoen Saduak floating market. Thai food is fantastic, too.

See you when you get back to Chicago.

Best regards,

Jim

2 Write a similar e-mail to a co-worker who is going to make a presentation in another city.

✉ **E-mail message**

Vocabulary check

Complete the sentences. Use the words in the boxes.

Units 1-3

| appointment | booth | conference | name | Pardon | presentation |

1 Good afternoon, Mr. Held. Here's your _____ tag and _____ bag.
2 _____ me, I'm looking for _____ 25.
3 Who's giving the _____ at the department meeting?
4 I have an _____ with Ms. Bell at 9:00 a.m.

Units 4-6

| acquaintance | borrow | factory | flight | make | motorcycles |

1 Yamaha makes _____ in a _____ near Batangas in the Philippines.
2 I met a business _____ on the _____ from Los Angeles.
3 Could I _____ your dictionary?
4 What _____ is your camera?

Units 7-9

| attend | come | deals | gift | make | jewelry |

1 I run the Production Department and _____ meetings.
2 He _____ with customer complaints.
3 I can't _____ it to the meeting tomorrow. Something has _____ up.
4 Is there a _____ store near here? I want to buy a _____ for my daughter.

Units 10-12

| change | delete | depart | fantastic | install | regards |

1 I'd like to _____ my reservation. I'd like to _____ on February the 5th.
2 Could you _____ this software on my laptop today?
3 Should I _____ this junk mail?
4 Thanks for a _____ trip. Please give my _____ to everyone at the New York office.

Answer key

1 Checking in

MODULE 1.1
1 Good morning. I'm Nathan Welsh. I'm with Dell.
2 Thank you.
3 Good afternoon.
4 Ah, yes, Ms. Gibson. Here's your name tag and conference bag.

MODULE 1.2
1 Good evening.
2 Good night!
3 Hello.
4 Good afternoon.
5 Good morning.

MODULE 1.3
1
1 My name's Carr. Jane Carr.
2 My name's Liu. Jia Liu.
3 My name's Kim. Da-Ye Kim.
4 My name's Harvey. Richard Harvey.

2 Students' own answer

MODULE 1.4
1

1 BP		2 ESPN		3 FIAT	
4 HP		5 HMV		6 IBM	
7 NEC		8 TDK			

2 Students' own answer

MODULE 1.5
1
1 I'm with / I work for Cathay Pacific.
2 I'm with / I work for CNN.
3 I'm with / I work for Daewoo.
4 I'm with / I work for Starbucks.
5 I'm with / I work for UPS.

2 Students' own answer

MODULE 1.6
1 Could you tell me your family name, please?
2 Could you repeat that, please?
3 Is that L-E-A-V-I-T?
4 And your given name?
5 Is that C-A-R-L?

MODULE 1.7

1 can		2 is		3 spell	
4 that		5 please		6 are	

MODULE 1.8
1 Could you spell that, please?
2 Could you fill out this card, please?
3 Here's your key card.
4 The elevators are over there.
5 Have a pleasant stay.

MODULE 1.9

Pierre	Hi, Emiko. It's Pierre.	8
Receptionist	Just one moment, please, Mr. Durand. I'll put you through.	5
Pierre	I'd like to speak to Emiko Takahashi, please.	2
Pierre	Thank you.	6
Receptionist	Good morning, TKE Engineering. How can I help you?	1
Emiko	Hello, Emiko Takahashi speaking.	7
Pierre	Durand. Pierre Durand.	4
Receptionist	Your name, please?	3

MODULE 1.10
1 a 4 b 1 c 5 d 3 e 2
2 Students' own answer

2 At a trade fair

MODULE 2.1

1 Where's		2 Thank		3 Excuse	
4 Aisle		5 café		6 Great	

MODULE 2.2

1 two		2 twelve		3 twenty	
4 thirteen		5 thirty		6 forty-five	
7 seventy-eight		8 ninety-nine			

MODULE 2.3
1 near the elevator
2 on the right, next to the restrooms
3 between the stairs and the elevator
4 across from the stairs
5 on the left, next to the stairs

MODULE 2.4
2 (Example answer)

A Where's your booth?
B It's in Aisle C. It's between the stairs and the restrooms.
A Ah. Booth 75?
B That's right.

MODULE 2.5
(Example answers)
1 The bookstore is on the left, between the business center and the restaurant.
2 The gift shop is on the right, next to the front desk.
3 The entertainment desk is on the left, near the restaurant.
4 The stairs are near the front desk.

MODULE 2.6
1 1 seven   2 six
2 Students' own answers

MODULE 2.7

2 1 T 2 F 3 T 4 T 5 F 6 F 7 T

3 Students' own answer

MODULE 2.8

1 Could I have your name, please?
2 What's your cell phone number?
3 Could you repeat that, please?
4 How do you spell that?

MODULE 2.9

Jane	Can you see the restaurant?	7
Jane	I'm in the restaurant. I just got here.	3
Jane	Hello, Kazuo?	1
Kazuo	Yes, I can. And I can see you! Bye!	8
Kazuo	Hi, Jane. Sorry I'm late. Where are you?	2
Kazuo	Yes, I'm in the meeting area.	6
Jane	It's next to the café. Are you in the Event Hall?	5
Kazuo	Where is the restaurant?	4

MODULE 2.10

Students' own answers

3 Schedules

MODULE 3.1

1 planning	2 morning	3 call
4 o'clock	5 time	6 afternoon
7 Thursday	8 What	

MODULE 3.2

S	A	L	E	S	X	P	M	P
T	S	C	I	O	C	E	I	R
A	E	U	T	S	M	Y	O	O
F	P	W	E	E	K	L	Y	J
F	U	O	A	C	U	C	S	E
Z	C	M	M	T	I	P	E	C
E	I	C	L	I	E	N	T	T
P	Y	S	U	O	P	Z	I	M
M	P	L	A	N	N	I	N	G

MODULE 3.3

1 Wed.	2 Thurs.	3 Fri.
4 Sat.	5 Sun.	

MODULE 3.4

1
1 4:00	2 2:15	3 11:25
4 7:20	5 1:45	6 6:05

2
1 five o'clock	2 five fifteen
3 eight twenty-five	4 three ten
5 nine forty-five	6 ten oh five

MODULE 3.5

2 1 Yes, there is. There's a section meeting in the morning at nine thirty.
2 Yes, there is. There's a production meeting in the afternoon at two fifteen.
3 No, there isn't.

MODULE 3.6

1
1 lunch	2 tour	3 session
4 presentation	5 demonstration	6 speech

2 Students' own answer

MODULE 3.7

2 Students' own answer

MODULE 3.8

Naomi	Hello, Steve. Am I calling at a bad time?	2
Steve	Around 3:15?	7
Steve	Hi, Naomi?	1
Naomi	Oh, I'm sorry.	4
Steve	That's OK, but can I call you back?	5
Naomi	Sure, that's fine. Speak to you then. Bye.	8
Steve	Well, I'm in a presentation right now.	3
Naomi	Sure, no problem. What time?	6

MODULE 3.9

Students' own answers

4 Companies

MODULE 4.1

1 work	2 makes	3 countries
4 with	5 Japanese	6 factories
7 famous	8 has	9 in

MODULE 4.2

2
1 Yes, she does.	2 No, it isn't.	3 Yes, it is.
4 Yes, it does.	5 Yes, it is.	6 No, it doesn't.
7 Yes, it does.	8 No, she doesn't.	

MODULE 4.3

1 BRAZIL
2 CANADA
3 EGYPT
4 FRANCE
5 RUSSIA
6 THAILAND

MODULE 4.4

1
1 New Zealand	2 Germany	3 Argentina
4 India	5 China	6 Italy

2 Students' own answers

MODULE 4.5

1
1 Korean	2 Swedish	3 Chinese
4 Japanese	5 French	6 American

2 Students' own answers

MODULE 4.6

1 Which company do you work for?
2 What nationality is your company?
3 Where is the head office?
4 Where does it have factories?
5 Where do you work?

MODULE 4.7

Students' own answer

MODULE 4.8

1
1 two hundred one
2 four hundred
3 six hundred fifteen
4 eight hundred fifty-eight

2
1 one hundred ten
2 three hundred sixty-two
3 five hundred thirty-seven
4 seven hundred forty
5 nine hundred ninety

MODULE 4.9

2
1 Bajaj Auto Ltd., Akurdi, Pune 411035, India

2 Rip Curl, 101 Surfcoast Highway,
Torquay, VIC 3228, Australia

MODULE 4.10

Vera	No, it's 723 Beacon Street.	4
Vera	7-2-3 Beacon Street.	6
Ted	I'm at the subway station. Is your address 733 Beacon Street?	3
Ted	723. Fine. See you soon. Bye.	7
Vera	Bye.	8
Vera	Hi, Ted. Where are you?	2
Ted	Hi, Vera. This is Ted.	1
Ted	Sorry, what was that?	5

MODULE 4.11

1
1 beef   2 coffee   3 sugar
4 steel   5 butter   6 wheat

2 Students' own answers

5 Meeting people

MODULE 5.1

1 meeting   2 flight   3 parking
4 Which   5 How   6 this
7 things   8 family   9 coffee

MODULE 5.2

1
Conversation 1
A Hello, I'm Karen Greenberg.
B Good to meet you, Ms. Greenberg.

Conversation 2
A Hello, Ms. Davis. How are you this morning?
B Pretty good, thank you. And you?

Conversation 3
A Hey, Joe, long time, no see!
B Yeah, it's been ages!

MODULE 5.3

2 Students' own answer

MODULE 5.4

1 Nyman   2 Jennifer   3 Jenny
4 Nokia   5 Marketing   6 Oboya
7 Edward   8 Eddie   9 Softech
10 Export

MODULE 5.5

1 Yes, that's right.
2 Nice to meet you, Ms. Okada.
3 Pretty good, thanks.
4 Not at all.
5 Good to meet you, Mr. Wada.
6 No, thanks, I can manage.

MODULE 5.6

1

Airline	Flight no.	Destination	Gate	Remarks
Air New Zealand	NZ 10	Honolulu	15	boarding
Singapore Airlines	SQ 286	Singapore	8	boarding
Qantas	AF 114	Sydney	11	boarding
Emirates	EK 435	Dubai	12	boarding
Pacific Blue	DJ 163	Raratonga	5	last call / boarding

2 (Example *answer*)
A Excuse me, what's the number of the Qantas flight to Sydney?
B AF 114.
A Thank you. And what's the gate number?
B Gate 11.
A Thank you very much.
B You're welcome.

MODULE 5.7

Brian	11:05. That's great. Which terminal?	2
Julia	Yes, I think so. 0190-320-9157.	7
Brian	VS 020. OK, see you at the arrivals gate. Do you have my mobile number?	6
Brian	That's it. See you tomorrow. Have a good flight!	8
Julia	Hi, Brian. I'm calling about my flight from San Francisco. I arrive at Heathrow at 11:05 a.m. tomorrow.	1
Brian	Terminal 3. Right. What's the flight number?	4
Julia	Terminal 3.	3
Julia	VS 020. That's Virgin Atlantic.	5

MODULE 5.8

1
1 f   2 d   3 a   4 e   5 b   6 c

2 Students' own answer

6 In the office

MODULE 6.1

1
1	for	2	ahead	3	lot
4	borrow	5	on	6	minute
7	run	8	any	9	problem

2 Students' own answer

MODULE 6.2

1	glue stick	2	flash drive	3	labels
4	paper clips	5	push pins	6	ruler
7	eraser	8	stapler	9	Post-its®
10	rubber bands		mystery word = calculator		

MODULE 6.3

1
apple 8		laptop 5	
books 4		notepad 9	
briefcase 14		pen 10	
calendar 7		phone 12	
camera 13		photographs 6	
coffee cup 3		plant 1	
keys 11		sandwich 2	

2 1 F 2 T 3 F 4 T 5 T 6 T 7 F

3
1 There's a briefcase under the desk.
3 There's a plant behind the laptop.
7 There are some books above the calendar / on the shelf.

MODULE 6.4

Students' own answer

MODULE 6.5

2 (Example answer)
This model is good for surfing the Internet and online gaming. It's medium-priced, very light, and battery life is excellent.

3 Students' own answer

MODULE 6.6

1	for	2	am	3	one
4	much	5	bit	6	very
7	is	8	not	9	think

MODULE 6.7

Sophie	Hi, Nazri. It's Sophie Milne.	2
Sophie	Five o'clock is fine. See you then. Bye.	8
Nazri	Tomorrow morning? Sure, no problem.	5
Nazri	Nazri Amar speaking.	1
Sophie	Could I use your laptop tomorrow morning? It's for my presentation.	4
Nazri	Hi, Sophie. What can I do for you?	3
Nazri	Bye.	9
Nazri	Sorry, I'm a little busy right now. Is five o'clock OK?	7
Sophie	Great, thanks. Can I pick it up now?	6

MODULE 6.8

1
1 file it, or shred it.
2 three pens on your desk.
3 drink at your desk.
4 at the end of the day.
5 plant on your desk.
6 in a desk drawer.

7 Work

MODULE 7.1

1	my	2	a	3	design
4	manager	5	large	6	visit
7	for	8	help	9	near
10	an	11	work	12	run

MODULE 7.2

Across
2	make	6	deal	7	visit
8	attend	11	sell	12	run

Down
1	call	3	write	4	help
5	give	8	read	10	design

MODULE 7.3

1 What do you do?
2 Which company do you work for?
3 What kind of company is it?
4 What do you do in your job?
5 Do you like your job?

MODULE 7.4

2/3 Students' own answers

MODULE 7.5

1 Margaret Rainer.
2 Gavin Benson.
3 The project meeting.
4 Three o'clock / 3:00 p.m.
5 Room 409.
6 Twelve.
7 The PowerPoint slides.
8 The projector.

MODULE 7.6

1 turn on / turn off / ~~shred~~	the air conditioner
2 copy / ~~unlock~~ / check	the price list
3 ~~print~~ / call / write to	Mr. Chang
4 ~~copy~~ / close / open	the door
5 install / delete / ~~call~~	the software
6 shred / copy / ~~turn off~~	the documents
7 recycle / ~~turn on~~ / read	the newspapers

MODULE 7.7

Takashi	Could I leave a message?	3
Anne	090-5551-7241. I'll give her your message.	6
Anne	I'm afraid she's not here at the moment.	2
Anne	Goodbye.	8
Takashi	Please ask her to call my cell phone number. It's 090-5551-7241.	5
Takashi	Thank you. Goodbye.	7
Takashi	Hello, this is Takashi Kondo of Nissan. Could I speak to Ms. Brewster in the Publicity Department, please?	1
Anne	Yes, of course.	4

MODULE 7.8

1
1. F – In New York, taxi drivers are usually men (99%).
2. T – In Vietnam, most agricultural workers are women (78%).
3. F – In the United States, nurses are usually women (92%).
4. T – In China, scientists and technicians are usually men (65%).
5. T – In the UK, primary school teachers are usually women (86%).
6. F – In Asia, most politicians are men (81%).

2 Students' own answers

8 Appointments

MODULE 8.1

1
1 speaking	2 do	3 want
4 meet	5 time	6 about
7 good	8 your	9 on
10 then		

2
1. Paul O'Connor.
2. The new website design.
3. September 15th.
4. Ten o'clock.
5. Mr. Viera's office.

MODULE 8.2

```
A  S  O  V  M  A  R  C  H  O  C
A  U  J  Y  J  A  N  U  A  R  Y  A
P  A  U  G  U  S  T  Y  T  V  F  F
J  R  S  O  N  Y  C  S  O  J  E  N
O  B  E  M  E  A  U  G  A  R  B  O
Y  E  P  C  Y  V  E  R  P  Y  R  V
O  C  T  O  B  E  R  S  R  M  U  E
C  T  E  S  Y  M  A  C  I  A  A  M
V  J  M  R  S  B  J  U  L  Y  R  B
E  C  B  Y  F  E  A  J  M  O  Y  E
M  F  E  D  E  C  E  M  B  E  R  R
O  E  R  S  T  T  C  B  R  A  U  O
```

MODULE 8.3

first – 1st	second – 2nd
third – 3rd	fourth – 4th
nineteenth – 19th	twentieth – 20th
twenty-first – 21st	twenty-second – 22nd
thirtieth – 30th	thirty-first – 31st

MODULE 8.4

Students' own answers

MODULE 8.5

1
| 1 1:20 | 2 6:59 | 3 5:05 |
| 4 8:32 | 5 3:10 | 6 9:40 |

2
1 four forty	2 seven twenty-three
3 two fifty	4 ten oh five
5 twelve thirty-five	6 nine twenty-five

MODULE 8.6

1
| 1 Junko | 2 advertising | 3 18 |
| 4 2 | 5 10 | 6 office |

2 Students' own answer

MODULE 8.7

1
1. OK, let's start.
2. Yes, the 18th is fine with me.
3. How about 9 a.m.?
4. How about 10:30?
5. Well, how about the small meeting room?
6. See you then!

2
Dear Ben and Chet,
It was good to talk to you today. Here are the details of the meeting:
topic – overtime
date – Friday the (19th)
time – (9 a.m.)
place – (large) meeting room
See you there!
Best wishes,
Amy

3
1. The meeting isn't on Friday the 19th, it's on Friday the 18th.
2. The meeting isn't at 9 a.m., it's at 10:30 a.m.
3. The meeting isn't in the large meeting room, it's in the small meeting room.

MODULE 8.8

John	Terrific. I'm really sorry about that.	7
Mark	That's too bad.	4
John	It's about our meeting this afternoon. I'm afraid I can't make it. Something's come up.	3
John	Hi, Mark. It's John.	1
Mark	Don't worry about it. Bye.	8
Mark	Hang on, I'll check. … Yes, tomorrow is fine.	6
John	Bye.	9
Mark	Hi, John. What can I do for you?	2
John	Can we make it tomorrow, same time?	5

MODULE 8.9

2 Students' own answer

9 Directions and shopping

MODULE 9.1

1. there; to
2. near; and
3. Excuse; from
4. me; of

MODULE 9.2

1 c   2 e   3 b   4 a   5 d

MODULE 9.3

2 (Example answer)

A Excuse me, is there a movie theater near here?
B Yes, there's one on Valley Road. Go along this street. Turn left at the second intersection. It's on the right, opposite the bank.

MODULE 9.4

1 two thousand
2 four thousand, five hundred forty
3 eleven thousand, two hundred eighty
4 four hundred twenty-nine thousand, six hundred
5 nine hundred eighty-seven thousand, eighteen

MODULE 9.5

1 1 dollars 2 euros 3 rupees
4 pesos 5 baht 6 pounds

2 Students' own answers

3 1 Ninety-nine dollars and ninety-**nine** cents
2 One hundred twenty-**six** thousand yen
3 **Twenty**-four thousand won
4 Five hundred **twenty** baht

MODULE 9.6

1 I'm looking for a bottle of perfume.
2 It's a gift for my wife.
3 That's a little expensive.
4 Would you like it gift-wrapped?
5 How would you like to pay?
6 Do you take visa?

MODULE 9.7

2 1 A watch. 2 No, it's for his daughter.
3 No, it's a little expensive. 4 Yes, it is.
5 Yes, he does. 6 No, he doesn't.
7 By credit card. 8 Yes, they do.

MODULE 9.8

Florist	Certainly. Large or small?	3
Florist	June 2018. Thank you. And just one more thing. The security number on the back?	7
Florist	Good morning, Mandy's Flowers. May I help you?	1
Carmen	Small, please.	4
Carmen	Yes, just a moment. It's 4591753662. And the expiration date is June 2018.	6
Florist	446. Thank you.	9
Florist	One small lily bouquet. Can I have your credit card number, please, Ms. Garcia?	5
Carmen	Yes, my name is Garcia. I'd like to order a lily bouquet for a birthday.	2
Carmen	The security number? Er … 446.	8

MODULE 9.9

1 1 cash 2 debit card 3 train card
4 credit card 5 PayPal 6 check

2 Students' own answers

MODULE 10.1

1 reserve 2 Which 3 or
4 see 5 like 6 time
7 quiet 8 room 9 many
10 from 11 double 12 Can

MODULE 10.2

1 1 Milano 2 four 3 Eight 4 Larsen 5 near

2 1 c 2 a 3 d 4 b

3/4 Students' own answers

MODULE 10.3

1 1 I'd like to make a flight reservation.
2 From Paris.
3 Seoul.
4 September 5th.
5 September 9th.
6 Just one.
7 Business.

2 Students' own answers

MODULE 10.4

1 September 25th and 26th. That's two nights.
2 From May 10th to 14th. That's four nights.
3 From July 2nd to 8th. That's six nights.
4 From August 12th to 16th. That's four nights.
5 October 10th and 11th. That's two nights.

MODULE 10.5

2 1 Sarah Cohen. 2 A hotel reservation.
3 No, a single room. 4 $120.
5 Three nights. 6 A quiet, non-smoking room.

MODULE 10.6

1 1 Economy 2 Premium
3 automatic 4 GPS / air conditioning
5 GPS / air conditioning

2 Students' own answers

MODULE 10.7

Michel	That's right. I'd like to change it to eight o'clock, if possible.	6
Manager	Just one moment, Mr. Picard. May I have your first name, please?	3
Manager	Good morning. Thai Garden restaurant. How may I help you?	1
Michel	Thank you very much. Goodbye.	8
Manager	Let me see. Yes, that's fine. So that's a table for two at eight o'clock. We look forward to seeing you this evening.	7
Manager	Goodbye.	9
Michel	Good morning. My name is Picard. I have a reservation for this evening.	2
Manager	Ah yes, Mr. Michel Picard. That's a table for two at 8:30.	5
Michel	Michel.	4

MODULE 10.8

2 Students' own answers

11 Requests and offers

MODULE 11.1

1 open	2 course	3 Thank
4 tell	5 Sure	6 Thanks
7 install	8 right	9 anyway
10 about	11 busy	12 later

MODULE 11.2

Across

3 turn	6 turn	7 mail
8 close	11 answer	12 make

Down

1 get	2 install	3 replace
5 write	6 open	10 check

MODULE 11.3

A Could you check the new website this afternoon?
B Sorry, I'm giving a presentation this afternoon.
A Ah, yes. Well, could you do it tomorrow morning?
B Yes, of course.
A Thanks.

MODULE 11.4

1 Jerry Weiss.	2 Vince Fox.
3 The Westech website.	4 The photographs.
5 Tomorrow morning.	6 The text.
7 Tomorrow evening.	8 Monday.

MODULE 11.5

1 Should I set up the projector?
2 Should I call the repair person?
3 Should I call you a taxi?
4 Should I get some sandwiches?
5 Should I recycle the newspapers?
6 Should I open the window?

MODULE 11.6

Students' own answer

MODULE 11.7

Jack	Oh, terrific. Thanks very much. I appreciate it.	7
Jack	Listen, could you check my computer?	3
Akira	Just a moment, I'll take a look. ... No, it's OK, it's off.	6
Jack	Akira? It's Jack.	1
Akira	No problem. Bye.	8
Jack	I think it's still on.	5
Akira	Hi, Jack. What's up?	2
Akira	Your computer? Sure. What's the problem?	4

MODULE 11.8

1 | 1 discount | 2 copy | 3 lend | 4 give |

2 (Example answers)
I think you can ask a senior co-worker "Could you give me some advice about my presentation?"
I think you can ask a co-worker and friend "Could you lend me some money for the coffee machine?"
I think you can ask a junior co-worker "Could you copy these documents for me?"
I think you can ask a sales clerk "Could you discount this camera?"

12 Socializing

MODULE 12.1

1 would
2 something
3 think
4 interesting
5 have
6 food
7 OK
8 about
9 love
10 near
11 would
12 at

MODULE 12.2

1 An iced coffee, please.
2 Yes, thanks. A chocolate chip cookie, please.
3 Two iced coffees and a chocolate chip cookie, please.

MODULE 12.3

1
1 amazing
2 terrific
3 fantastic
4 great
5 wonderful
6 exciting

2 Students' own answer

MODULE 12.4

1 I'd love to, but this Sunday is a bit difficult.
2 What about a game next Sunday? That's the 16th.
3 Yes, the 16th is fine. I'll look forward to it.
4 I'd love to, but tomorrow's a bit difficult.
5 How about the day after tomorrow?
6 Thursday? Yes, that's good for me.

MODULE 12.5

1 Students' own answers

2 (Example answer)
A Do you like Korean food?
B Yes, I love it.

MODULE 12.6

(Example answers)

A There's a nice French restaurant near my office.
B That sounds wonderful.

A There's an excellent Thai restaurant in our building.
B That sounds good.

MODULE 12.7

1 can
2 in
3 OK
4 make
5 is
6 then

MODULE 12.8

Students' own answer

MODULE 12.9

Barbara	My pleasure. Have a good trip.	4
Jung-Soo	Hello, Barbara? It's Jung-Soo.	1
Jung-Soo	Yes, I will. Ah, we're boarding. Thanks again, Barbara. Bye.	7
Jung-Soo	Thanks. It'll be good to get home.	5
Barbara	Bye.	8
Jung-Soo	Yes, I'm at the departure gate. Thank you very much for everything.	3
Barbara	Oh, hi, Jung-Soo. Are you at the airport?	2
Barbara	And give my regards to everybody at the Seoul office.	6

MODULE 12.10

2 Students' own answer

VOCABULARY CHECK

UNITS 1–3

1 name; conference
2 Pardon; booth
3 presentation
4 appointment

UNITS 4–6

1 motorcycles; factory
2 acquaintance; flight
3 borrow
4 make

UNITS 7–9

1 attend
2 deals
3 make; come
4 jewelry; gift

UNITS 10–12

1 change; depart
2 install
3 delete
4 fantastic; regards